GMC
Gazette • Media • Company

Published by Gazette Media Company Limited, Gazette Buildings, Borough Road, Middlesbrough TS1 3AZ. Tel 01642 245401. Fax: 01642 210565. Printed by Juniper Publishing, Juniper House, 3, Sandy Lane, Melling, Liverpool L31 IEJ

ISBN 0-9528814-6

Contents

Cover photos: Front - Hullo Bridge, near Middleham
Back - High Green, Great Ayton

Foreword

Dedicated to Joan,
my walking companion.

THERE are many varied rural landscapes within easy travelling distance of Teesside and each has its own identity, with footpaths which draw me back time and time again.

Each route has its own special memories - memories of superb views, of outstanding buildings, wild flowers, bird-song and unexpected sightings of wildlife, such as the stoat I spotted in a hedgerow near Kirkby-in-Cleveland.

Our climate is full of surprises too, and it's important to make simple preparations in terms of stout footwear and waterproof clothing along with a small amount of food and drink.

Most of the routes in this selection are clearly waymarked along well-defined paths, making it easier to follow the Country Code as we savour the delights of the varied land-scapes between the rivers Esk and Wear.

- Bob Woodhouse

About the author

BOB Woodhouse has been writing, broadcasting and lecturing on aspects of local history for the past 30 years.

An early interest in the countryside and the rich history of the North-east was fostered by Alan Falconer, who wrote the Rambler column in the Evening Gazette for many years and was also the author's history teacher at Acklam Hall Grammar School in Middlesbrough.

Bob has literally followed in his mentor's footsteps by becoming a regular contributor to the columns of the Evening Gazette over a period spanning two decades.

After spending almost 30 years in teaching, he retired from full-time work in December 1994 in order to pursue research and writing projects.

He now lives in Middlesbrough and is currently working on several aspects of North-east history as well as on a novel set in Cleveland during the early nineteenth century.

Commondale & Castleton

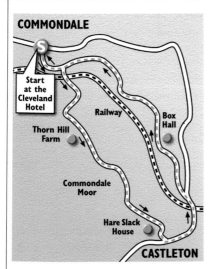

NORTH YORK MOORS

Making tracks in beautiful Eskdale

Start: Cleveland Inn, Commondale.

Distance: 5.5 miles.

Going: Fairly severe in places, notably sectors approaching and leaving Castleton.

Refreshments: Cleveland Inn, Commondale & venues in Castleton.

Map: Ordnance Survey Outdoor Leisure 26: North York Moors western area.

Walk Facts

S EVERAL of the Eskdale villages are linked by footpaths on either side of the river - with superb views of the surrounding landscapes on all sides.

Starting from the Cleveland Inn at Commondale, we bear right past Chapel Garth on the left to follow the lane that leads to the railway station. We soon pass the red-brick Ness Terrace and walk down the sloping roadway towards Foul Green.

As the road bears right we continue directly ahead on the bridleway past Foul Green House and soon reach a white-walled cottage. The track runs uphill but we pass through the gate and walk across a small field to reach a ladder stile. We continue along the bottom edge of the field and cross the stile before making our way over the railway track and across the field that leads to a footbridge.

On the other side of the River Esk the path runs up the hillside to a ladder stile and then along the left of the field towards Westgate Farm. Waymarkers guide us towards a stile and we then walk diagonally to the left towards a ladder stile, before following the field edge directly ahead.

We can see houses at Castleton on the skyline as we pass over two stiles and keep to the left of farm buildings at Thorn Hill Farm.

A very muddy track runs between a fence and wall to reach a stile and the pathway then veers to the left and then right to cross a beck. We soon cross two more stiles and then walk halfway up the field to reach a set of stone steps over the wall.

Heading up the field towards farm buildings, we turn left down the lane between stone walls and along a track close to the top of the field. After passing through the gap, we keep close to the stone wall and after about 50 yards bear right over a wooden stile and through shrubs to a farm track.

Turning left down the slope we pass between the farm buildings with Rose Cottage close on the left and head down the grassy slope. At the bottom the path veers to the left and after about 25 yards we head to the right beside the hedge.

A wooden footbridge leads across the beck and after following the waymarked route along the field edges we reach the public roadway. After crossing the road we head up the slope into Castleton and turn left along the High Street to pass No.62 High View on the left.

Continuing down the High Street we can pick out the school and Co-operative Store on the left and the Methodist Chapel on the right. Just after No.2 Wayside we bear left down the slope and walk down the hill to cross the bridge over the Esk. As we follow the road up

Commondale - looking towards the Cleveland Inn

the slope we soon pass the Eskdale Hotel and then Dunorlan House. At the top of the hill the road bears right but we follow the bridleway off to the left.

The wide stony track runs downhill past Winnow Hall and Box Hall and then uphill into birch woodland. We soon reach a wooden field gate and follow the wide track past the white-walled bungalow through to Foul Green and then back up the public road to our starting point.

Glaisdale & Egton Bridge

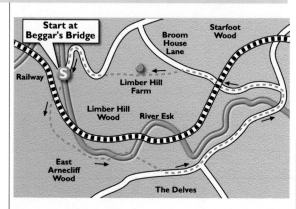

Start at Beggar's Bridge

Starfoot Wood

Broom House Lane

Railway

S

Limber Hill Farm

Limber Hill Wood

River Esk

East Arnecliff Wood

The Delves

Walk Facts

NORTH YORK MOORS

A historic feast for lovers of legends

Start: Beggar's Bridge, Glaisdale.

Distance: 3.5 miles.

Going: Moderate with severe gradients in places.

Refreshments: Venues in Glaisdale and Egton.

Map: Ordnance Survey Outdoor Leisure 27: North York Moors eastern area.

EACH of the villages along the River Esk has its own delightful setting and a selection of fascinating characters from the past. Nowhere is that more true than at Glaisdale and Egton Bridge.

Starting from Beggar's Bridge at Glaisdale, it's worth pausing to take in the natural beauty of the Esk Valley and the story that is linked with this fine packhorse bridge.

Tom Ferries, a local lad with little wealth, was forbidden from marrying his sweetheart, who lived across the river in the days before there was a bridge, and left the area in search of a fortune. He returned several years later with considerable wealth, married the young lady and provided money to finance construction of the bridge and other local projects.

After passing under the railway bridge, we cross the footbridge and then head to the left up the hillside into East Arncliff Wood. There are glimpses of the River Esk below on the left as the path rises and falls through the sloping woodland. For much of the way the route is along a paved causeway and wear on the stones shows just how much it has been used by our ancestors!

The path runs out of the woods to meet the public road at Delves and at this point we turn left to make our way downhill towards Egton Bridge. Continuing along the public road, it bends sharply to the left to cross the Esk and it's worth taking a closer look at the nearby St Hedda's Roman Catholic Church.

As well as admiring a magnificent interior, we can also find details of the life and work of Father Nicholas Postgate. Born at nearby Kirkdale House in 1599, he trained as a priest and ministered to local Roman Catholic families. But in the late 1670s a ruthless campaign was waged against Catholics and Father Postgate was detained at Littlebeck where he was about to conduct a service of baptism. Conviction at York Assizes was followed by gruesome execution at Tyburn but his influence throughout Eskdale continues today.

We follow the riverside road away from Egton Bridge and under the railway bridge into Broom House Lane. After passing the buildings of Broom House Farm on the right we leave the public road and make our way into the field on the opposite side of the roadway.

Keeping to the left-hand edge beside the woodland we make our way down the slope to cross the beck and then head up the

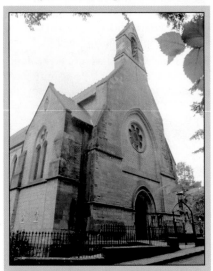

hillside and over a stile into an area of coniferous woodland. Beyond the wood, the path runs beside the left-hand wall and a set of farm buildings soon comes into view. On the approach to Limber Hill Farm, we bear left along a narrow strip of land to reach a gate next to the roadway.

Turning left along the road, we make our way down the severe gradient of Limber Hill to reach our starting point at Beggar's Bridge.

St Hedda's Church, Egton Bridge chronicles the life and work of Nicholas Postgate

Romantic link: Beggar's Bridge, Glaisdale

Lastingham Circular

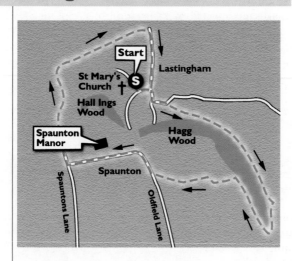

NORTH YORK MOORS

A rich variety of moorland contrasts

Start: The Blacksmith's Arms, Lastingham.

Distance: 4.5 miles.

Going: Moderate gradients through woodlands and fields.

Refreshments: Blacksmith's Arms, Lastingham.

Map: Ordnance Survey Outdoor Leisure 26: North York Moors western area.

THERE is such a lovely mixture of rolling hillsides, open moorlands and varied woodland on this walk which makes this area one of my favourite locations for a North Yorkshire stroll.

Starting from the Blacksmith's Arms opposite Lastingham Church, we bear left into the village and soon cross the little bridge over Ings Beck. St Cedd's Well is on the left as we continue through the village to pass the Methodist Chapel on the left and follow the roadway eastwards past Coromoor House.

Just after Gander Green, we leave the road to follow a footpath between trees and round to the right to reach a stile. After about 40 yards we cross another stile and a stone-flagged footbridge leads over the beck before the pathway follows a well-worn route above a gully on the left.

Starting point: The Blacksmith's Arms at Lastingham

We soon reach another stile at the edge of the woodland and then walk across an open field with trees on both sides. At the metal field gate, Hagg Wood is on the right and we keep to the top edge of the fields as we walk through to the public road.

Turning right up the slope, we turn right just before the summit on a footpath that leads into Hagg Wood. The path soon leaves the wood to run along a sloping field and the route

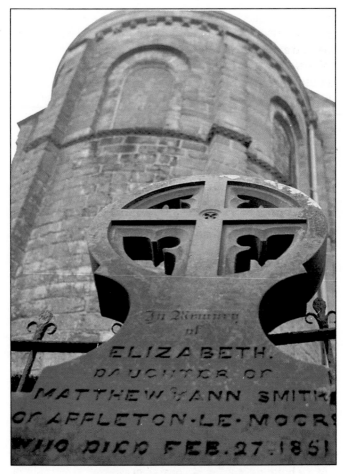

St Mary's Church, Lastingham

then rises gently to pass between lines of trees. The woodland path runs on down a slope but we bear left through a gap into the field and follow the right-hand edge.

Turning right along the next field for about 40 yards, we then turn left to follow the right hand field edge through a gate and diagonally across the next field to reach Oldfield Lane next to the pond.

We bear right along the roadway and, at the junction, turn left to follow the public road into Spaunton. Woodman's Cottage is prominent on the right as we continue through the village to turn right at the junction.

We soon pass Grange Farm on the left and, at the bottom of the hill, we bear left on the road to Hutton-le-Hole. After about 100 yards, a track runs away to the right with allotments close at hand on the right. After crossing a stile, the route runs beside a hawthorn hedge and across a small beck.

The right of way bears to the right and, as we approach the buildings of Camomile Farm, our route veers left around the trees. There are fine views across the open moors as we follow the stone wall down the slope and over Hole Beck.

Continuing up the slope, we cross a swampy area to reach a kissing gate and stile and, at the top of the hill, there's a seat - with splendid views on all sides.

At the signposts we follow the wall round to the right and, after passing through a field gate, we join the roadway that runs past Lastingham Grange Hotel on the left and The Old Orchard on the right. As we continue down the slope, Tranmire and West View are close at hand on the right - with St Oswald's Well on the left.

At the bottom of the hill, we bear right and walk back through the village to our starting point at the Blacksmith's Arms.

Osmotherley North

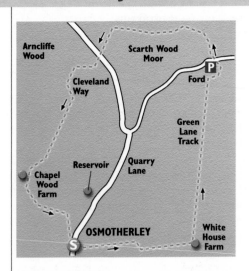

Arncliffe Wood

Scarth Wood Moor

Cleveland Way

Ford

P

Green Lane Track

Reservoir

Quarry Lane

Chapel Wood Farm

OSMOTHERLEY

White House Farm

S

Walk Facts

<u>NORTH YORK MOORS</u>

Stunning views from a walker's mecca

Start: The Market Cross, Osmotherley.

Distance: 4.75 miles.

Going: Moderate to severe gradients.

Refreshments: Venues in Osmotherley.

Map: Ordnance Survey Outdoor Leisure 26: North York Moors western area.

OSMOTHERLEY has become a sort of mecca for walkers, hasn't it? That's no surprise really - with so many alternative routes and superb views on all sides. This slightly longer stroll covers a range of scenery from open moors to woodland.

Starting from the Market Cross in Osmotherley, we cross to the war memorial and then make our way through the passageway to pass the Methodist chapel of 1754. Continuing past Bramblewick, we cross Back Lane and follow the Cleveland Way between wooden fences to reach a long flight of steps and a gravel path leading down the slope to a wooden footbridge.

The route then runs uphill past White House Farm and, at the junction with Green Lane, we turn left up the slope. An uneven surface makes walking difficult in places and it's worth pausing to take in some superb views away to the left.

There are clumps of gorse and bracken on both sides of a level stretch and after passing through a field gate and then a kissing gate, we continue directly ahead into a wooded area. At the end of the coniferous woodland, a ladder leads over the stone wall on to South Wood Moor.

We walk directly ahead for about 25 yards and then bear to the right between areas of heather to join High Lane. Turning left along the trackway, we follow the slope down to a footbridge at the popular location known as Sheepwash.

We continue directly ahead and cross the roadway to follow the left-hand verge towards Scarth Nick. As the hillsides open up there are views of industrial Teesside and just before the road signs we bear left to follow the bridleway up the hillside.

There are fine views of Whorl Hill, Swainby and Roseberry Topping as the track veers to the left to rejoin the Cleveland Way. As the walkway rises gently, Scarth Wood Moor is close at hand on the left and large stone slabs have been set into the route to prevent erosion. After crossing two stiles, we walk beside woodland to reach the BT microwave radio station at a height of 982 feet above sea level and, away across the open moors on the left, we can see the Bilsdale Mast.

The track runs downhill along the edge of South Wood and then twists and turns through old quarry workings before running directly downhill. At the foot of the hill we bear left to pass through a kissing gate and after a second gate we bear left as the track divides close to Chapel Wood Farm.

Osmotherley: the Market Cross and War Memorial

As we walk up the gravelled trackway there's a stone plinth on the left showing landmarks away to the west. The track on the left leads to the Lady Chapel but we continue ahead with the slopes of Rueberry Hill on the left.

There are properties on both sides as we follow Rueberry Lane through to the junction at the northern end of Osmotherley. Turning right we make our way back down the hill to our starting point at the Market Cross.

Sandsend & Lythe

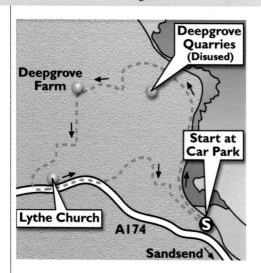

Deepgrove Quarries (Disused)

Deepgrove Farm

Start at Car Park

Lythe Church

A174

Sandsend

S

Walk Facts

<u>**NORTH YORK MOORS**</u>

On the right line for spectacular coastal views

Start: Car park at the foot of Lythe Bank.

Distance: 3.25 miles.

Going: Several moderate to severe gradients.

Refreshments: Venues in Sandsend.

Map: Ordnance Survey Outdoor Leisure 27: North York Moors eastern area.

S OMEWHAT quieter times have returned to Sandsend since the closure of the coastal railway line and the former track now offers the chance to take a look at old alum workings and enjoy some superb coastal views.

Starting from the car park at the bottom of Lythe Bank, we walk away from the roadway and up the steps to join the old railway track. There are views of the bare headland to the north and ledges of rock cover the foreshore away to our right.

Trees line the slope as we pass between gorse bushes and continue directly ahead - taking in views of the bay. There are shale tips from old alum workings on both sides as the embankment runs high above the rocky bay and we then head through a cutting towards a rocky cliff face.

The track veers left and at the bricked-up tunnel entrance we bear to the right and make our way up the steps through wood-land - with a wooden rail in places for those needing some assistance. At the top of the steps we bear right for a few yards and then cross the stile and head to the left along the edge with the fence on the left.

There are arable fields on both sides and fine sea views as we cross another stile to continue along the cliff edge. At the next stile we head to the left away from the cliff edge - with the fence on the right. We soon reach a field gate and a waymarker directs us to the right towards Deepgrove Farm.

A signpost close to the junction of paths directs us to the left along a gravel track and we walk between farm buildings to reach a wooden gate. The path runs across the field to the bottom right-hand corner of the field where we make our way down a short flight of stone steps and through a bridle gate into the wood.

Continuing through the wood, we head along a stone trod to

A tranquil riverside scene at Sandsend

reach a gate and stile. Walking directly ahead along the track we soon reach the A174 - with Lythe Village close at hand on the right.

We turn left along the main road and it's worth a closer look at Lythe Church. Its tower is a landmark for miles out to sea and the interior houses stonework from earlier buildings on the site as well as memorials to the Phipps family from nearby Mulgrave Castle.

Leaving the churchyard, we bear left down Lythe Bank as far as a field gate on the left, then head diagonally left down the field to cross two stiles before bearing right above the old quarry workings.

We turn left down a series of flights of steps through the quarry and great care is needed where the steps are steep with tricky bends as we follow the track downhill to join the former railway line. Turning right along the wide trackway we retrace our steps back towards the old station buildings and then left down the steps that lead back into the car park.

The tower of Lythe Church can be seen from miles out to sea. The interior stonework is worth a close look

Borrowby & Cod Beck

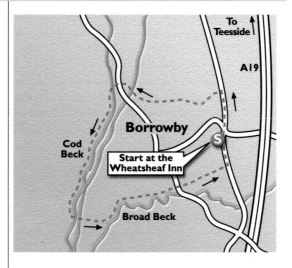

NORTH YORKSHIRE

Where rolling countryside is at your Beck and call

Start: The Wheatsheaf Inn, Borrowby.

Distance: 4.75 miles.

Going: Mainly level with inclines at start and finish.

Refreshments: Wheatsheaf Inn, Borrowby.

Map: Ordnance Survey Landranger 99: Northallerton, Ripon and surrounding area.

T HE spreading village of Borrowby covers high ground to the north of Thirsk - with lovely views across rolling countryside away to the west beyond Cod Beck.

Starting from the Wheatsheaf Inn at the centre of Borrowby, we walk in a northerly direction up the sloping roadway past Hollydene on the left and Pear Tree House on the right.

An old pump makes an interesting roadside feature as we continue along the main road through the village and, after passing Hanami on the left, we turn left along St Helen's Lane.

This sunken roadway runs between hedges past St Helen's Cottage on the left and bends to the left as it runs downhill to

**The village of Borrowby enjoys lovely views across
rolling countryside to the north of Thirsk**

Our route follows the line of Broad Beck

reach the public road where we turn right. Walking along the roadway we can soon make out the buildings of Old Hall Farm and, after crossing a narrow road bridge, the metalled road veers left over another bridge. At this point we turn left through a metal field gate to follow the raised riverbank beside Cod Beck.

The right of way soon joins a track and we follow this route past an old farm building and modern bungalow on the left.

There are several metal field gates and smaller metal gates along this stretch - with Cod Beck close at hand on the left. A range of farm buildings - Crosby Grange - comes into view on the hillside away on the right and, opposite the farmstead, we cross a concrete footbridge over Cod Beck.

After about 60 yards we cross another concrete footbridge before following the left-hand edge of the field to a stile with Broads House on the left.

Our route then runs diagonally to the right across the next field to a stile just past the telegraph wires and then veers left towards Broadbeck House.

The footpath follows the line of Broad Beck - with several stiles and a small wooden gate - through to the public roadway where we turn right towards Knayton. After about 60 yards we turn left over a stile next to the metal gate and walk along the edge of the field to another stile before crossing a field.

Beyond the next metal field gate we cross another stile, then walk between a line of hedges on both sides to join a lane that runs through to the main road opposite Three Chimneys.

Turning left up the roadway we pass a number of attractive properties on both sides - including Weavers Cottage and Field House on the right and Little Stokesley on the left - on the way back to our starting point at the Wheatsheaf Inn.

Great Ayton & Aireyholme

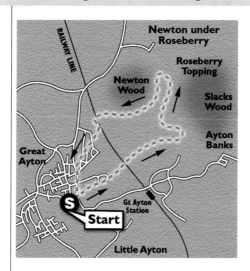

NORTH YORKSHIRE

Following in the footsteps of Captain Cook

Start: Northern end of High Green, Great Ayton.

Distance: 3.75 miles.

Going: Some moderate/ severe gradients on outward section.

Refreshments: Various venues in Great Ayton.

Map: Ordnance Survey Outdoor Leisure 26: North York Moors western area.

GREAT Ayton is an ideal starting point for following in the footsteps of the young James Cook. As well as the site of the Cook family's cottage - adjacent to Easby Lane - and the schoolroom where James spent his early years, there's now a fine sculpture of a youthful James Cook on the High Green.

Walking towards the northern end of High Green we pass the Royal Oak on the left and make our way round the bend into Newton Road.

After just a few yards we cross with care and pass through a kissing gate to walk across the field with the buildings of Cleveland Lodge ahead on the left. The track soon runs through a small wooded area and then continues along the left hand edge of the field to reach the railway crossing.

As we continue over a stile next to a metal gate and beside the wire fence, there are fine views of the Cleveland Hills away on the right. The path soon veers to the left to reach a stile at the lower edge of Cliff Ridge Wood and it's worth taking a look at the National Trust information panel with details about Cliff Rigg Quarry.

From this point we walk up the steep slope on the right and soon pass two concrete sections dating from mining days. At the top of the slope we reach a stile with a tall signpost and make our way round the right hand edge of the field over two stiles to join the roadway that leads to Aireyholme Farm.

We follow the metalled road to the left to pass the buildings of Aireyholme Farm and continue directly ahead with views of Roseberry Topping away on the right.

Keeping to the left of the cottage we reach the brow of the hill - with industrial Teesside covering the low ground away in the distance - and then bear to the right to cross several stiles as we make our way up the lower slope of Roseberry Topping.

JAMES COOK
who lived in Great Ayton
between 1736 and 1745
later became
Captain James Cook R.N F.R.S
Famous Navigator

The young James Cook surveys Ayton's High Green

A plaque on the wall informs us that the ornate shooting box was built by Commodore Wilson of Ayton Hall in the late 18th century. Just beyond the lodge we bear left down the grassy slope and the path soon bends to the right to reach the bottom of the hill where we turn left to follow a muddy track along the bottom edge of Newton Wood.

Aireyholme Farm

After crossing a couple of wooden footbridges the path rises and falls as it runs through the woodland and, when the path divides, we bear right along the lower route. We can pick out St Mary's Church at Nunthorpe across open ground on the right and after joining a rough track we turn right to cross the railway bridge.

Immediately after the bridge we turn left to walk beside the hedgerow with the railway track below on the left. At the end of the section of hedge we cross a stile on the right and continue across two fields with Cliffe House close on the right to reach houses lining Roseberry Crescent. We turn left along the roadway before bearing to the right down Roseberry Drive.

At the next junction we bear left and within a few yards turn right along a footpath that runs behind the houses to link up with Newton Road. Bearing left along the roadway we continue round the right hand bend to return to our starting point on High Green.

Kirkby-in-Cleveland

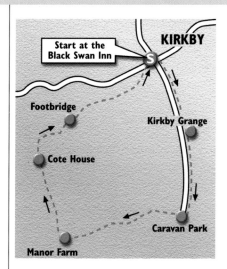

KIRKBY

Start at the
Black Swan Inn

S

Footbridge

Kirkby Grange

Cote House

Caravan Park

Manor Farm

Walk Facts

<u>**NORTH YORKSHIRE**</u>

Ancient and modern within sight of the Tees

Start: The Black Swan Inn, Kirkby-in-Cleveland.

Distance: 3.75 miles.

Going: Lengthy uphill section at the start.

Refreshments: Black Swan Inn, Kirkby-in-Cleveland.

Map: Ordnance Survey Outdoor Leisure 26: North York Moors western area.

L OCAL volunteer groups have improved paths and foot-bridges in the Kirkby area to open up a network of routes with superb views on all sides.

Starting from the Black Swan at Kirkby-in-Cleveland, we head south along Kirkby Lane towards the hills. The old school house - dating from 1688 - is on the opposite corner but there are several modern properties on both sides of the roadways as we make our way up the sloping roadway.

Rutland House on the left, and Cranimoor on the right contrast with the solid stonework of Hill View - and, sure enough, there are fine views of high ground below Cold Moor and the distinctive outlines of the Wainstones along this next stretch. We soon pass Kirkby Lodge on the left and a roadside seat celebrates Queen Elizabeth's Coronation in 1953.

The modern brick-built property, Adenbrook, is prominent on the right while a cluster of farm buildings make up Kirkby Grange on the opposite side of the road. After climbing steadily over the first section, the roadway levels out as we approach the foot of the hills and there are caravans in the field on our

The Black Swan, Kirkby-in-Cleveland

right hand. The Pybus Centre for Boy Scouts is directly ahead but we turn right along the road leading to Toft Hill Farm Caravan and Camping Park. After crossing a stile before the farm buildings, we keep to the left-hand edge of the field and it's worth pausing along this section to take in some fine views of the Cleveland Hills away to the right and central Teesside on lower ground to the north.

Continuing through a gap in the fence the ground is extremely muddy and there's another stile on the other side of the narrow field. We walk directly ahead towards a small wood and, after about 50 yards, we cross a stile before walking along the bottom edge of the field to reach a wooden footbridge.

Waymarkers guide us over two more stiles and another footbridge as we head towards Manor Farm. There are four more stiles before we reach the farmyard where we bear right along the roadway.

Following the gently sloping road, we pass to the right of buildings at Cote House and after passing a large holly bush on the left, we look for a stile in the hedgerow on the right.

The path follows the bottom of the field to reach a concrete bridge with metal rails and then runs through a strip of woodland to cross another bridge before running above the beck on the left.

After the next stile, a flight of steps leads to another bridge and beyond the next stile we walk diagonally to the left before crossing the roadway that leads to Dromonby Farm away on the right.

Continuing directly ahead over the stile in the hedgerow, we soon cross a track and follow the field edge to the left-hand corner where the path veers to the right to cross another footbridge and nearby stile.

We can see the rear of properties directly ahead and we make our way through to Kirkby Lane where we turn left to return to our starting point at the Black Swan.

Hutton Rudby & Sexhow

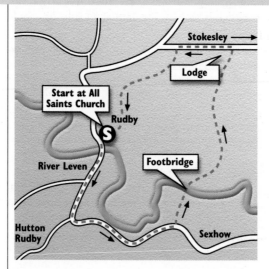

Stokesley →

Lodge

Start at All
Saints Church

Rudby

S

River Leven

Footbridge

Hutton
Rudby

Sexhow

Walk Facts

NORTH YORKSHIRE

A gentle stroll around a delightful village

Start: All Saints Church, Hutton Rudby.

Distance: 3.5 miles.

Going: One or two moderate gradients.

Refreshments: Venues in Hutton Rudby.

Map: Ordnance Survey Outdoor Leisure 26: North York Moors western area.

HUTTON Rudby is an ideal location for a gentle stroll - through a delightful village setting and rolling country-side with fine views of the Cleveland Hills.

Starting from All Saints Church beside the River Leven, we follow the pavement on the right-hand side of the roadway as it runs uphill past the Bay Horse on the right. As the road bears right, we cross with care to pass the Wheatsheaf on the left and walk directly ahead past Hutton House.

The Wynd is prominent on the right and at this point we leave the roadway to follow a track that runs down a slope with walls on both sides.

The track soon veers to the left to join the public roadway that runs downhill - with a seat on the left - and across a bridge before climbing towards farm buildings at Sexhow Hall.

As the road bears right before the farm we turn left to cross a stile and then follow the track downhill with farm buildings on the right. Towards the bottom of this slope we bear right to reach a metal foot-bridge with a wooden

The Wynd, Hutton Rudby

deck next to the fir plantation. After crossing, we continue up the right-hand edge of the field. Opposite the farm buildings on the left, we bear right through a wooden kissing gate and walk directly ahead along the verge between fields.

As the field starts to slope downhill we follow the verge away to the left to reach a fence on the right and, by following the fence round to the left, we soon reach a wooden stile.

After crossing the stile there is a metal fence on the right and, as we continue ahead, an avenue of trees soon runs across the field from the left. Opposite the trees we cross another stile and then turn left to reach a metal kissing gate that leads along the driveway towards a lodge.

We pass through the gate on the right to reach the public road and then turn left up the slope. At the top of Folly Hill, opposite some metal sheds, we cross the road and pass through a metal gate - taking care to shut it firmly.

As the track veers to the left towards the farm buildings we bear to the right across the grass to reach a stile. Within 20 yards we cross another stile close to a metal gate.

Hutton Rudby lies on lower ground as we walk directly ahead to a gap in the hedge at the bottom of the field and continue down the slope to reach a metal gate and stile.

Following the right of way across the field, we continue along the bottom of the field passing a stile on the right and walk behind houses and gardens to reach a stile in the right hand corner next to some evergreens.

Care is needed as we make our way down the slope through woodland to cross a wooden footbridge over the beck into the churchyard. Following the flagged pathway to the left of the church there are fine views of the River Leven and weir as we return to our starting point at the lych-gate.

The weir on the River Leven at Hutton Rudby

Nunthorpe & Newton
-under-Roseberry

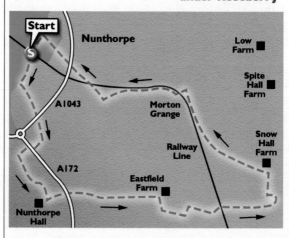

**NORTH YORKSHIRE**

Peace and quiet on Teesside's doorstep

Start: Nunthorpe Station.

Distance: 6.5 miles.

Going: Level almost all the way.

Refreshments: King's Head, Newton-under-Roseberry.

Map: Ordnance Survey Outdoor Leisure 26: North York Moors western area.

ONE benefit of living on Teesside is that there is so much fine countryside on the doorstep - with quiet paths through level countryside that has the Cleveland Hills as a dramatic backcloth.

Starting from Nunthorpe Station on Guisborough Road we walk in a westerly direction to pass Nunthorpe and Marton Recreation Club on our left. Just after passing The Avenue on the right we turn left away from the roadway to follow the path between fences to cross a stile at the corner of the field.

Walking directly ahead, we soon cross another stile on the right and bear left to reach a stile in the hedgerow overlooking the A1043 Nunthorpe bypass. After crossing with care, we continue ahead to reach a kissing gate that leads into the churchyard.

St Mary's Church, Nunthorpe

Bearing to the right through the churchyard we pass through the lych-gate and walk down Church Lane to the junction with the A172 Stokesley Road. We turn right and walk towards the roundabout where we bear left along the lane which runs towards Grey Towers Farm.

Just before the farm we turn left along the tarmac roadway that soon passes Grey Towers Court and after crossing the section of woodland on the left we head over a stile in the metal fence and down the sloping field to join the Old Stokesley Road next to the gas installation.

Walking into Nunthorpe village, we leave the roadway just before the farm buildings and follow the sloping track down to the A172. After crossing with care, we walk ahead to Eastfield Farm and opposite the farm buildings we turn right through a field gate.

At the next metal field gate we turn left - with a wire fence on the left - and walk ahead to reach a wooden footbridge. Following this field edge round to the left we pass through a metal gate in the corner of the field and then walk round the right-hand edge of the next field to pass under a railway bridge.

We walk directly ahead towards Newton-under-Roseberry with fine views of Roseberry Topping as a backcloth and, at the public road, we turn left to pass St Oswald's Church.

"Lych Garth" is on the right as we follow the roadway round the bend and ahead towards Snow Hall Farm. Continuing to the right of the farm buildings, we walk behind the main lock and between sheds to pass through a metal gate and along a track to reach the bottom of the slope.

At the gate we walk ahead to the right-hand corner of the field and after crossing a stile our route runs ahead for some 25 yards to reach a wooden footbridge on the left. Continuing

The view from Nunthorpe towards Roseberry Topping

across the next field to the top left-hand corner we cross another stile and bear diagonally left to reach another stile close to the railway embankment.

After crossing the railway line the path runs beside a fence to yet another stile. We keep to the right-hand field edge - with Morton Grange on the left - and after the next gate and stile we join a gravel track that runs beside the railway line.

At the junction of tracks we bear right along Morton Carr Lane and after crossing the railway line the track veers to the right to reach the A1043 Nunthorpe bypass. After crossing with care we follow the lane past St Mary's Church Hall and through to the junction with Guisborough Road where we turn left to return to our starting point at Nunthorpe Station.

Askrigg

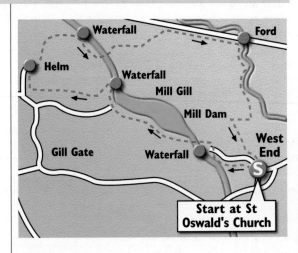

Waterfall

Ford

Helm

Waterfall

Mill Gill

Mill Dam

West End

Gill Gate

Waterfall

S

Start at St Oswald's Church

Walk Facts

THE YORKSHIRE DALES

Gills and waterfalls in Herriot country

Start: The Parish Church of St Oswald.

Distance: 3.5 miles.

Going: Moderate gradients through woodland and fields

Refreshments: Various venues in Askrigg.

Map: Ordnance Survey Outdoor Leisure 30: Yorkshire Dales northern and central area.

A SKRIGG, between Leyburn and Hawes, was noted at one time for its clockmakers, but now it's the James Herriott connection and some fine local waterfalls that bring visitors to this pleasant Wensleydale village. It was here, not Herriott's Thirsk, in which All Creatures Great and Small was filmed. The series still brings in the crowds.

Starting from the splendid parish church of St Oswald in the market square, we follow the roadway round to the left and make our way along West End past Lynburn Cottage.

The roadway soon narrows and then bends between houses before becoming a lane. After passing the single storey Tute Hill on the left, we go through a gate on the right - with a sign to Mill Gill Force.

A paved trod runs across the field to a gap in the wall - next to the old mill - and the route then follows the stream for a short distance as far as the footbridge. On the other side of the bridge, the path continues to the right and soon runs up a short flight of steps before following the stone wall on the left.

When the path splits, it's worth making the short detour down the sloping path on the right to take a look at Mill Gill Force. After returning to the junction, we follow the main path uphill - with the wall on the left - and then head left over the wall at the signpost to Helm.

As we follow the right hand edge of the field, there are fine views across Wensleydale and, after passing through another gap in the wall, we continue along the top of the field and through to the road close to Helm.

We turn right along the road and soon pass three houses close at hand on the left before veering to the right to walk in front of Helm Country House. As we follow the gravel pathway, look out for the dovecot on the front of the country house.

Our route then runs up the right hand side of the field and, at the signpost to Askrigg via Low Straights, we bear right along the ridge. After dropping down the slope to the beckside, we follow Whity Gill as far as the steps over the wall and then continue up the stony slope. After the next gap in the wall, we bear right on a well worn path that runs high above the beck before dropping down to a footbridge.

On the other side of the beck, we head up the slope and soon reach a signpost to Low Straights. Passing through the metal gate, we join the farm track and make our way uphill - with views of Askrigg Church below on the right.

At the junction of tracks, we bear right and follow the slope downhill between stone walls on either side. Just before the ford, we pass through the metal field gate on the right and continue across the field. We keep close to the beck and pass through a gap beside the barn as we continue down the slope.

There are gates on the gaps in the wall on both sides of the lane and, after yet another field gate, we walk directly ahead to pass through a narrow wooden gate at the bottom of the field. The route runs out onto the roadway and, after turning left we continue along West End to return to our starting point at the church.

The Wensleydale village of Askrigg was the location for the filming of All Creatures Great and Small

Guisecliffe Circular

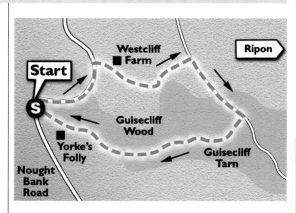

THE YORKSHIRE DALES

Natural beauty and one man's folly

Start: Parking area for Yorke's Folly on Nought Bank Road, south of Pateley Bridge.

Distance: 3.5 miles.

Going: Moderate gradients. Keep to main path on approach to Yorke's Folly (potholes amongst heather).

Refreshments: Pateley Bridge

Map: Ordnance Survey Land Ranger 99: Northallerton, Ripon and surrounding area.

THERE'S a real mix of scenery on the south side of the River Nidd between Pateley Bridge and Glasshouses - with man-made features contrasting with the natural beauty.

Starting from the roadside parking area for Yorke's Folly, on Nought Bank Road to the south of Pateley Bridge, we walk in a northerly direction down the sloping roadway with evidence of quarrying operations on both sides.

As the road bends to the left, we bear right on a track that is signposted to Glasshouses. The level track runs past a cottage on the left hand side and then passes another imposing property - Far High Westcliffe - on the way to a wooden field gate.

Continuing along the gravel track, we pass through a metal field gate and, as the route bends between trees, there are fine views across the Nidd on the left - with woodland covering slopes on the right.

As the track veers towards a metal field gate, we turn right to walk beside a stone wall and soon reach a wooden field gate that leads into Parker Wood. Passing between holly bushes and clusters of silver birch trees, there are outcrops of rock beside the pathway as we make our way up the slope.

The path reaches a level stretch and, at the junction of routes, we bear right on the wider route that runs up the slope. At the next level section, we veer to the right to take a look at Guisecliff Tarn. Leaving the tarn, we continue ahead up a stony bank and, at the summit, the path runs down through woodland before sloping uphill again to reach open ground.

There are superb views across Glasshouses away to the right and, as the path splits, we bear right up the slope towards the radio mast. After crossing the ladder stile, we turn right and walk beside the stone wall until the track veers to the left.

It is important to keep to the pathway of the Nidderdale Way at this point as there are potholes and pits left by quarrying operations among the heather on both sides.

We soon reach another ladder stile and continue directly ahead with a stone wall on the right-hand side towards a third ladder stile complete with dog flap.

Yorke's Folly - originally built with three towers in the 1700s, but now known locally as the Two Stoops

The pathway then reaches Yorke's Folly. During the late 1700s, local benefactor John Yorke was so concerned about unemployment levels that he organised construction of the monument. Originally it had three columns, but one blew down during a gale in 1893 and the structure is now known locally as the Two Stoops. From this vantage point there are superb views-from Whernside in the west across to the Yorkshire Wolds in the east.

The last section of our route runs directly ahead down the sloping trackway back to our starting point at the roadside parking area on Nought Bank Lane.

Leyburn & Wensley

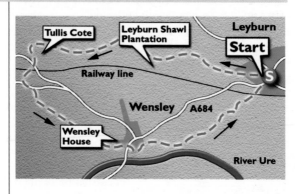

THE YORKSHIRE DALES

A landscape which inspired artists

Start: Leyburn Town Hall, Market Place.

Distance: 5 miles.

Going: Moderate slopes through fields.

Refreshments: Various venues in Leyburn.

Map: Ordnance Survey Outdoor Leisure 30: Yorkshire Dales northern and central areas.

L EYBURN nestles on a hillside overlooking Wensleydale and a delightful stroll to the nearby village of Wensley offers some superb landscape views.

Starting from Leyburn Town Hall in the market place, we cross the A684 to make our way into Commercial Square. Keeping to the left, we follow the narrow lane up the slope from Commercial Square and along to the open hillside known as the Shawl.

There are superb views across the valley from this natural limestone terrace and it's no surprise to learn that this fine natural setting inspired a local man, Fred Lawson, to set up the Bolton Group of artists in the 1930s.

It's easy walking for the most part along a well-defined pathway, passing through kissing gates and step-through stiles, with seats at several points to take in the views. A variety of trees including yews and firs, oaks and sycamores shade the route in places but we can make out extensive quarries away on the right.

After leaving Leyburn Shawl Plantation, the pathway slopes to the left; after crossing two stiles, we make our way into a large field. There's another stile as we approach farm buildings

Our circular route takes us past Leyburn church

at Tullis Cote and, just past the farm, we turn left as our route runs down a slope with Wensley Brook on the right.

Bearing to the right, we cross the public road and, after making our way through a field gate, we continue over the railway line before crossing a field that leads to the public roadway. We turn left and walk along the road for about 150 yards before turning right into woodland.

The path runs to the left - with woods on the right - and we follow the field edge to join a track that runs down the slope to link up with a driveway close to Wensley House. Turning left along the drive, we soon reach the A684 in Wensley village where we bear right towards the church. We walk along the road beside the church and, after crossing the beck, turn left past Glebe Cottage. The lane veers to the right and on the bend a field gate has an inscription relating to 'Italian PoW 1944'.

Walking across the field, we soon reach a stile and follow the bottom edge of the field under power lines to yet another stile.

The path then runs up the field edge with a wire fence on the right and beside the left hand side of the woodland. The second stile along this stretch leads to Leyburn Old Glebe Field and, after crossing a wooden footbridge, there are several gaps in field walls as we continue directly ahead - with views of Middleham away on the right.

After crossing two arable fields, we bear diagonally to the left to cross a stile before the barn and the pathway crosses several more stiles then runs up the left hand field edge.

We can see houses on the ridge and, after the next stile, we walk diagonally across the field to reach a ladder stile next to the rail track. Continuing over the next field, we pass through a gap and make our way up to the public roadway. Turning right along the road, we follow the bend back to our starting point.

Middleham & Hullo Bridge

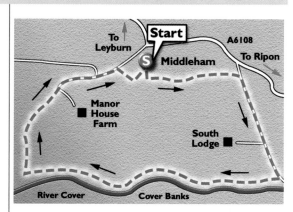

To Leyburn · **Start** · A6108 · **To Ripon** · **Middleham** · **Manor House Farm** · **South Lodge** · **River Cover** · **Cover Banks**

Walk Facts

THE YORKSHIRE DALES

A land of legends, castles and noble steeds

Start: Middleham Market Place.

Distance: 4.5 miles.

Going: Moderate hill climb on return section.

Refreshments: Various venues in Middleham.

Map: Ordnance Survey Outdoor Leisure 30: Yorkshire Dales northern and central areas.

THERE'S a real sense of history around the cobbled market place of Middleham in the Yorkshire Dales, near Leyburn.

Perhaps it's that splendid castle and its links with King Richard III or those galloping steeds that remind us of the sport of kings. Whatever the reason, this fascinating village is set in some delightful countryside that's well worth exploring.

Starting from the sloping market place, we walk up the hill towards the castle and then continue along the level section of Corvan Lane - with the castle on our right. Away on the right is William's Hill - an early motte and bailey castle built during the late 11th century as a base for Ghilpatrick the Dane.

Legend says that if you run round the hill seven times, a door will open to reveal great treasures - and who's going to doubt this unlikely tale after the recent discovery of the Middleham Jewel!

As the track begins to rise, there's a gate on the left and after passing through, we continue directly ahead between tall hedges on both sides. We soon reach a stile and, after crossing, the path runs directly ahead - with the football and cricket fields on the left. After passing through a gap in the stone wall, we continue over the brow of the hill before veering to the left to make our way down the slope towards the left-hand corner of the field.

At the gap in the wall, we pass through and turn right along Straight Lane. There are stone walls on both sides and, as the track veers to the right, we continue directly ahead along the grassy lane that leads to the riverbank.

Close to the bank, we turn right to cross the fence, with a line of stepping stones spanning the River Cover on our left. After passing through an area of woodland, we reach open meadows

The cobbled market place of historic Middleham

with a line of trees on the opposite riverbank. At the next gate, we head up the sloping stony track and, as it levels out, the fallen trees are a reminder of earlier storms.

High cliffs are prominent on the opposite side of the river and the path then wends its way through woodland to reach another stile. We continue along the riverbanks and at the next stile a waymarker directs us up the sloping hillside on the right.

A gully runs up the right-hand edge of this large field and after walking as far as the first ridge, we bear left to follow the bottom edge of the field around the strip of riverside woodland at Cover Banks. A stile on the left leads into a large sloping field and we continue down the gentle gradient towards the stonework of Hullo Bridge.

After taking in the views of some delightful scenery, we head away from the bridge and back up the hill along the right-hand edge of the field. There are two gates near the top of the hill as we approach the roadway at Coverham Lane and, at the roadway, we turn right to walk along the broad grassy verge.

As we get near to the village, a waymarker directs us across the field on the right and on the opposite side of the field we cross the wall and turn left to follow Corvan Lane back past the castle and into the market place.

Our route takes in delightful scenery like this at Hullo Bridge on the River Cover

Reeth & Grinton

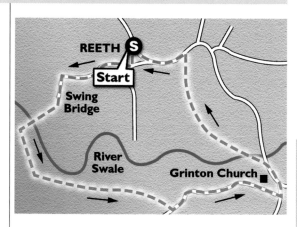

THE YORKSHIRE DALES

Swale and hearty along the riverside

Start: National Park Centre, Reeth.

Distance: 3.5 miles.

Going: Moderate gradients iin places.

Refreshments: Venues in Reeth and Grinton.

Map: Ordnance Survey Outdoor Leisure 30: Yorkshire Dales northern and central areas.

S WALEDALE is many people's favourite walking country and there are plenty of delightful strolls between riverside villages.

When you've savoured the views and places of interest around Reeth's sloping village green, walk down the gentle gradient on the south side - with the King's Arms on the right. We soon pass the National Park Centre (formerly the Literary Institute) and then follow the track that runs to the left of Holmlea Cottage and passes Hilary House on the right. At the junction of lanes, we bear right - following the sign to Swing Bridge - and continue past Wraycroft Cottages on the left.

There are tall stone walls on both sides of the narrow lane, as we continue past the doctors' surgery and Quaker Garth. A seat on the right looks out across the Swale and a stony pathway drops down to the left - with farm buildings on the right.

The pathway then runs through a wooden field gate towards the river and after crossing a plank bridge on the right, we head along a well-worn path to the swing bridge.

Dales delight: a super view on the way from Reeth to Grinton

After crossing, we bear left - noting the shoals of riverside pebbles and debris from earlier flood levels. There are superb views of the surrounding countryside as we follow the path beside a wire fence to reach a wooden field gate next to a metal field gate.

Keeping to the left-hand edge beside the fence, we soon reach a wooden field gate and beyond the gate the pathway has a stony surface as it runs towards yet another wooden gate.

After making our way down a sloping section, we continue along a level stretch to pass through a wooden gate and the river is now close at hand on the left. There's another seat on the right for those in need of a rest and the well worn path now continues directly ahead to a metal gate.

We turn left along the metalled roadway - taking care on the bends - and soon see the tower of Grinton Church directly ahead. As we reach Mill House on the right, we bear left into the churchyard. St Andrew's Church - with everything on the grand scale - is a reminder that although the nearby village is small, the parish extends for miles.

At the other side of the churchyard, we reach the roadway and turn left to pass the Bridge Inn which is across the road on the right. Continuing across the road bridge, there's a "Slow" sign on the road surface and at this point we bear left through the wall and down a short flight of stone steps. The track then runs across the level field and through a kissing gate to continue beside the river.

Passing a group of farm buildings on the right, we continue directly ahead to the public road and then turn left to cross the narrow road bridge - with great care!

We follow the road past Bridge House on the right as it runs back to the green at the centre of Reeth.

Tranquil Reeth at the heart of Swaledale

Barnard Castle & Flatts Wood

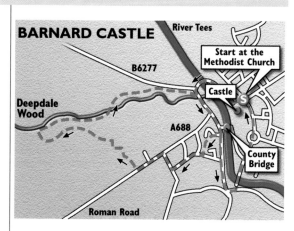

Walk Facts

TEESDALE & THE RIVER TEES

The best of all worlds at Barnard Castle

Start: Methodist Church at junction of Galgate and Horse Market.

Distance: 4.25 miles.

Going: Several moderate - severe gradients.

Refreshments: Several venues in Barnard Castle.

Map: Ordnance Survey Landranger 92: Barnard Castle area.

BARNARD Castle has the best of both worlds - splendid buildings and lovely local countryside - and this stroll combines both facets.

Starting from the Methodist Church at the junction of Galgate and the Horsemarket we walk down the sloping pathway with the entrance to the castle on the left.

Inside the imposing walls, the castle grounds are divided into four wards with most of the stonework dating from the period 1250-1350 and the Great Chamber and Round Tower the most impressive buildings.

As the path veers to the left, the old gasworks site has been re-styled with an interesting stone and brick feature but we turn right to follow a sloping track that runs down to the riverbank. Continuing ahead to the pipe bridge, we cross the Tees - pausing in the centre of the bridge to take in fine views of the castle - and then turn left along the B6277.

We soon cross a road bridge and, after passing Flax Field on the left, the site of Ullathorne Mill offers further dramatic views of the castle walls. Just before the county bridge we cross the road with care and turn right away from the roadway to follow a path on the left hand side of Number 3. The path slopes uphill and before the railings we turn left along a flagged way and then cross a side road to reach a wooden gate in the stone wall. A flagged way runs across the sloping field to another gate where we turn right to follow a gravel path behind a row of houses and through to the roadway.

Turning right, we soon pass Beech Cottage and Startforth Lodge on the right before reaching the junction with the A67 at the Royal Star Inn. We turn left up the hill and soon cross Corn Close and Stainmore Close on the left to reach Startforth Park on the opposite side of the road.

Barnard Castle views: looking towards the castle from the site of the former gas-works and the iron bridge over the River Tees

A footpath sign on the roadside directs us into the housing estate and we follow the main route through the houses into a cul-de-sac. In the left-hand corner of the roadway a footpath runs beside the fence and behind houses to cross a narrow beck before turning left around the fence of the Young Offenders' Institution.

The stony track continues round to the right before turning away from the fence to cross a beck close to a stile. Keeping close to the fence, we bear right to another stile and then make our way into the woods.

Our path runs along the top edge of the woodland and, after crossing a narrow gully and nearby stile, we bear right between gorse and holly bushes. The pathway continues away to the right over an expanse of springy open grassland and then runs down the slope to join the lower path beside the Deepdale Beck.

Turning right, we soon pass a low waterfall - with a wire fence on our right. After dropping down to the riverbank, there is a simple stone-built shelter on our right.

At the wooden footbridge we cross the beck and, just before the ford, our route runs to the left to cross another footbridge over Gill Beck.

Turning right, we follow the wide track that runs through to the B6277 where we cross with care and retrace our steps past Flax Field and County Bridge.

We follow the riverside roadway past the White Swan but, as it veers to the right, our route runs beside the river and along to the footbridge. After crossing, we follow the roadway back up The Bank past Blagraves House on the right and continue along the Market Place to return to our starting point at the Methodist Church.

Gainford & Park House

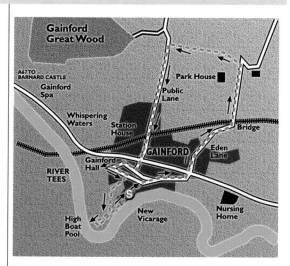

Walk Facts

TEESDALE & THE RIVER TEES.

The going's easy but beware the currents

Start: St Mary's Church, Gainford Green.

Distance: 3 miles.

Going: Easy on field paths and pavements.

Refreshments: Several venues in Gainford.

Map: Ordnance Survey Landranger 93: Cleveland and Darlington.

THE delightful Teesside village of Gainford and the nearby countryside are worth a closer look at any time of year. Starting from St Mary's Church on Gainford Green, we walk along the south side past the Vicarage before crossing the open grassy area.

A short flight of steps leads to the frontage of the Academy Theatre where we bear right to pass the village Post Office. Continuing along Tees View, we reach the Lord Nelson on the corner and cross the A67 with care before bearing right and then left into Eden Lane.

Robin's Court is on the left - with Eden Park on the right - as we follow the gently sloping roadway northwards. The road soon bends to the right and then sharply left to cross an old railway bridge.

Walking directly ahead, we keep to the right of a tall hedge and follow the footpath beside a wooden fence with views of Park House among trees away on the left. The path soon crosses a plank bridge over a beck and we then turn left - with a wooden fence close at hand on the right.

Continuing directly ahead, we soon cross a stile next to a wooden field gate and there are two more gates before we reach a section of the track that runs between a stone wall on the right and a hedge on the left.

The pathway leads to the public road where we turn left towards Gainford. We soon pass Hill Crest and Tynecot on the left and Great Wood on the right as the tarmac footpath runs down the slope.

The new housing estate at Balmer Hill on the right contrasts with the old stone-built terraces of West View on the left and we can pick out the former railway platform and building as we reach Station Court.

Walking along North Terrace, we cross the A67 with care and continue directly ahead along the side road before turning right into High Row past the Cross Keys on the corner.

At the end of this fascinating roadway we turn left to pass Gainford Hall and, as the road levels out, we can see the Coach House prominent on our right hand side.

After a right turn into School Lane, the school buildings are on our right and further along

Beware the treacherous currents on this stretch of the Tees near Gainford

this quiet roadway we pass Edleston House on the left and the cemetery on the right. At the metal gates we pass through the central gap and bear right towards the riverbank.

It's worth pausing at the bend in the river to take in some lovely scenery around High Boat Pool - but the Tees has some treacherous currents at this point and it is important to keep both feet on firm ground.

Returning along the riverside path, we follow a gravel slope into the churchyard and, if time allows, it's worth taking a closer look at the splendid interior of St Mary's Church.

High & Low Coniscliffe

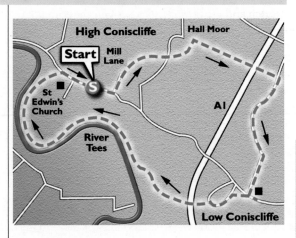

Walk Facts

TEESDALE & THE RIVER TEES

A country stroll close to the motorway

Start: The Spotted Dog Inn, High Coniscliffe.

Distance: 4.25 miles.

Going: Easy on level field paths and tracks.

Refreshments: The Spotted Dog or Baydale Beck Inn.

Map: Ordnance Survey Landranger 93: Cleveland and Darlington.

THERE'S a variety of scenery on this stroll on the western edge of Darlington - with farmland on the outward stretch and the river landscape of the Tees on the return section. Starting from the Spotted Dog at High Coniscliffe, we turn left away from the A67 down Mill Lane. There are tennis courts on the right and bungalows on the left as we head towards Mill House.

Passing through the gate and over the beck, we follow the beck for a short distance before veering away to the right across the field. Look out for a stile where the fence joins the stone wall and, after crossing, follow a track between arable fields. There are farm buildings on the right as we continue directly ahead.

The route is waymarked and, after crossing the first stile, there are several step-through stiles before we reach a track that leads to Hall Moor on the left. Heading towards the red brickwork of Hall Moor, waymarkers direct us away to the right across the field and then along successive field edges until we reach a gravel trackway.

The sound of motorway traffic is prominent in the near distance - the buildings of Coniscliffe Grange are on the far side of

St Edwin's Church at High Coniscliffe

the A1 - as we bear right to cross a bridge over the carriageways of the A1. A stile on the first bend leads to a pathway along the edge of the field and we soon reach a wide track. Turning right, we follow the track down a gentle slope - with fine views directly ahead across the countryside.

Following the track through to the A67, we bear left and soon pass the Baydale Beck Inn on the left. After crossing the road, we climb a stile in the roadside hedge and follow the pathway across the field towards houses at Low Coniscliffe.

Walking between two properties, we reach the public road and bear left through Low Coniscliffe. It's possible to pick out one or two of the earlier properties among more modern housing and it's interesting to see how river boulders have been used in walls and houses.

At the western end of the village we follow the roadway round to the right and then make our way over a stile next to a gate and continue over the A1(M). The track runs directly ahead between the fields - with farm buildings on the left - to reach the riverbank.

Turning right, we follow the well worn track of the Teesdale Way as it runs upstream towards High Coniscliffe. The path soon bends to the left and then runs through a strip of woodland - with plenty of wildflowers and birdsong.

Away on the right, we can make out the spire of St Edwin's Church at High Coniscliffe and, after crossing a stile, we continue ahead through a sloping grassy area. There's a shoal of river boulders on the left and, as the river channel veers to the right, we can see the buildings of Holme House on the far bank.

Continuing along the raised track, we head up the slope beside the church to reach the A67. Our starting point at the Spotted Dog is a short distance away on the right.

Staindrop

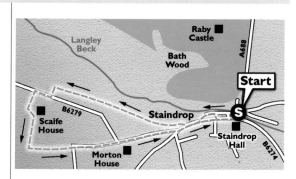

TEESDALE & THE RIVER TEES

History comes alive on a walk back in time

Start: St Mary's Church, Staindrop.

Distance: 4.5 miles.

Going: Easy with one moderate gradient.

Refreshments: Venues in Staindrop.

Map: Ordnance Survey Landranger 92: Barnard Castle area.

STAINDROP is proud of its close links with nearby Raby Castle and many of the village's buildings show the influence of the Vane family in recent centuries.

St Mary's Church has been enlarged several times but it is still possible to trace Saxon windows and roof lines above Norman arches in the nave and much of the tower dates from the Norman period. The west end of the church houses some impressive alabaster effigies of the Neville family.

Leaving the churchyard we walk along Front Street to pass Staindrop Hall on the left and the Royal Oak on the right before turning right into Barnard Street. At the end of the road we turn left and, with Langley Beck on our right, we soon pass Wood View and Westfield Paddock.

Continuing directly ahead between stone walls we pass Moidart and follow the narrow lane round to the left beside Mill Wynd. This pathway soon reaches the Green where we turn right to pass the police station on the right - with a quoits pitch in front.

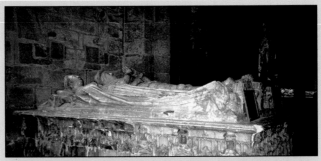

**This alabaster effigy of Ralph, 1st Earl of Westmorland
can be seen inside St Mary's Church at Staindrop**

Next to No 54 - at the entrance to Lady Close - we follow the footpath between properties and through a gap in the wall to walk directly ahead with a hedge on the right and wire fence on the left.

A stile leads into a field where we bear left to reach a metal gate and wooden stile and then continue along the field edge to a stone wall and step.

Keeping close to the high stone wall around Raby Park we cross two more sets of steps before we reach a white-walled bungalow. Our route runs directly ahead beside the wall as far as a house and gate where we turn left along the wide trackway that runs down a track to the main B6279 road.

We turn right along the road and, after crossing with care, we turn left up the track that leads to Scaife House. The right of way runs through the farmyard and round to the right before veering left into the adjacent field through a gap next to a wooden fence.

We walk directly ahead down the field and, after crossing the beck, we continue through a gap to make our way across a second field. At the wooden field gate we bear right to follow the field edge and continue around the edge as it bears to the left to reach a metal field gate on the right.

Passing through the gate, we follow the right-hand field edge to another metal field gate where we turn left along a wide lane. The lane soon veers to the right and then runs directly ahead to join the B6279 close to Morton House.

After crossing with care, we continue directly ahead to the junction with the A688 at the west end of Staindrop. Then we make our way back through the village - taking a closer look at some of the prominent buildings such as Malvern House - as we return to our starting point at St Mary's Church.

St Mary's Church, Staindrop

Whorlton & Abbey Bridge

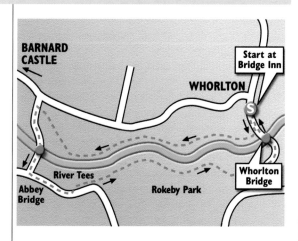

Walk Facts

TEESDALE & THE RIVER TEES

History comes alive on a walk back in time

Start: The Bridge Inn, Whorlton.

Distance: 6 miles.

Going: Mainly level with gradients on return sector.

Refreshments: The Bridge Inn, Whorlton.

Map: Ordnance Survey Landranger 92: Barnard Castle area.

A SLIGHTLY longer stroll - just downstream from Barnard Castle - takes in some of the loveliest river scenery along the River Tees.

Starting from the Bridge Inn at Whorlton, we walk in a southerly direction along the Green to reach the former red-brick vicarage building. Just past the Whorlton sign, we turn right to follow a pathway beside a brick wall - with the river below on the left.

The route is waymarked, with a series of stiles to negotiate as we make our way along the edge of several fields and through a stretch of woodland. Away on the right we catch glimpses of buildings at Sledwich Hall and at this point the pathway runs along a stony stretch before sloping down to a footbridge.

Continuing up the steps on the other side of the bridge, we make our way along the field edge with views of Mortham Tower across the river on the left. Yet another stile leads into a large field and we head towards a set of steps over the wall in the top right-hand-corner.

Continuing across the next field, we pass close to a large tree in the centre then veer left to reach another set of steps over the wall. On the other side we head to the left to walk beside the wall - with woodland on the left and an arable field on the right.

At the next stile, a waymarker directs us into the woodland and, after crossing the beck, we make our way through a canopy of trees taking care to step over fallen tree trunks along the way!

After crossing another stile, we continue along the pathway to a gate and then follow the path beside a stone wall with the public road on the left. Next we pass through a gate on the left, heading down the road to cross Abbey Bridge and it's worth pausing, as we cross, to take a look at the picturesque Tees gorge below the bridge.

Immediately after the bridge, we turn left to follow the Teesdale Way through woodland. A gravel path runs gently downhill to reach a stile and stepping stones over the Manyfold Beck. The path then runs round the field edge before heading into more woodland. We soon reach the public road and turn left to cross the bridge over the River Greta.

From this point we can see the Meeting of Waters where the rivers Tees and Greta join - a setting that has attracted countless artists down the years.

After crossing a cattle grid, we head up the track towards Mortham Tower before heading to the left to cross a stile in the fence. Continuing along the level stretch at the top of the field, we cross another stile and pass through a wooden gate before reaching a metal gate. At this point we veer to the left down the sloping field to reach steps set in the roadside wall.

We turn left to cross Whorlton Bridge and, next to the old toll house, a long flight of steps leads back up the hill and directly ahead is our starting point on the Green at Whorlton.

Whorlton Bridge on the loveliest stretch of the Tees

Brandon Circular

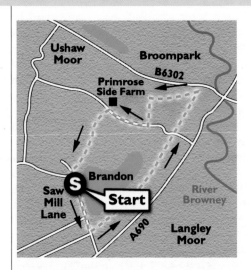

Walk Facts

WEARDALE & THE RIVER WEAR

Memories of mining and the age of steam

Start: The Prince Bishop public house, Brandon.

Distance: 4.5 miles.

Going: Mainly level with one moderate uphill gradient on return approach to Brandon.

Refreshments: The Prince Bishop, Brandon village.

Map: Ordnance Survey Landranger 93: Cleveland and Darlington.

IN RECENT years the East Durham landscape has changed dramatically as railway lines and coal mines have given way to rolling fields and pleasant walkways - but amidst some fine spreading panoramas, it's still possible to pick out traces of our industrial heritage.

Starting from the Prince Bishop public house in Brandon village, we walk in an easterly direction down the slope of Sawmill Lane and pass a row of stone-built cottages before reaching a garage on the left-hand side.

We soon turn left along the tarmac surface of the Brandon - Bishop Walkway and between a gap in the hedges we can make out school buildings close at hand on the left. Crossing the public roadway, we continue directly ahead as the pathway dips and bends between evergreens with houses on the right-hand side. At the end of the housing we cross another pathway to walk into an open area - with Meadowfield Sports Centre and St John's Church clearly visible on the right-hand side.

The gravel track runs round a fenced sports pitch on the left and we soon leave the housing and adjacent sports club to walk down a slope between trees and through to the public road.

After walking 30 yards to the right we cross with care and continue along the gravel pathway with woodland on the left and an arable field on the right.

The next stretch of the walkway runs high above fields on both sides and we can clearly see the main east coast railway line on the right before dropping down a slope to the footbridge with metal rails over the River Deerness.

Bearing left up a steep slope we reach a trackside seat at the junction of the Lanchester Valley, Deerness Valley and Brandon Bishop Walkways. At this point we turn left along the

Lanchester Valley Walk and as the pathway runs high above fields on the left, there's a picnic area on the right.

As the landscape levels out we make our way into a cutting with silver birch trees on both sides and after passing under a former railway bridge, we turn left up a slope that leads to the approach to the bridge.

We turn right to walk down the slope between wire fences and after making our way down a flight of stone steps, we cross a wooden footbridge with metal sides. We walk up the slope and after a left-hand bend we reach the public road.

Turning right along the roadside pavement we head downhill and then up the hill to reach Primrose Side Farm on the right. Opposite the farm buildings we head left over a stile and walk up the right-hand field edge to reach a kissing gate.

There are two stiles before we follow the right-hand field edge round to another stile and the route then follows a track through to the roadway at North End in Brandon village. We turn left up the public road to pass the Bay Horse on the right and our starting point at the Prince Bishop is a short distance away on the left.

The River Deerness and the East Coast main line

Tunstall Reservoir

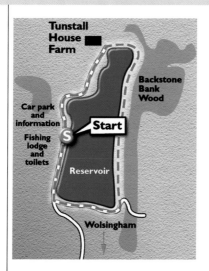

Tunstall House Farm

Backstone Bank Wood

Car park and information

Start

S

Fishing lodge and toilets

Reservoir

Wolsingham

WEARDALE & THE RIVER WEAR

Woodland wildlife by the water's edge

Start: Car park next to fishing lodge at northern end of reservoir.

Distance: 2.5 miles.

Going: Undulating paths.

Refreshments: Venues in Wolsingham (2 miles S).

Map: Ordnance Survey Landranger 87: Hexham, Haltwhistle & surrounding area.

C ONSTRUCTED in 1879 by the Weardale and Shildon Water Company, Tunstall Reservoir - two miles north of Wolsingham in south-west Durham - has been in continuous use since then to supply the Bishop Auckland and Shildon areas.

Starting from the car park next to the Fishing Lodge at the northern end of the reservoir, we return to the roadway and turn right to cross a stone bridge over the beck. Just after the right-hand bend, we cross a stile next to the wooden gate and then bear left along the edge of the reservoir. A tall holly bush is prominent on the bank side and the next section of the reservoir is edged with stone boulders to prevent erosion.

After passing another holly bush we can see patches of erosion along the riverbank and the path continues across a plank bridge to follow the edge of the reservoir - with a wooden fence on our left-hand side.

A ladder stile leads over a smart stone wall with the buildings of Tunstall House Farm prominent on the left. We bear to the right along a wide trackway and soon cross a stone bridge with Waskerley Beck leading into a nature reserve.

An information panel gives details of animal and plant life that is found close by - including the thread rush, a wiry tufted perennial growing ten inches high, that was first discovered at Tunstall Reservoir in 1970.

At the end of the stone wall - before a wooden field gate - we bear to the right over a ladder stile to make our way into Backstone Bank Wood.

This lovely area of oak woodland has been designated as a Site of Special Scientific Interest by English Nature and the well-worn pathway soon runs over a little stone footbridge before rising above the reservoir - with woodland covering the

Testing the waters at Tunstall Reservoir

slope away on our left. A section of wooden fencing runs round a large tree and the path then follows stepping stones over the beck before running up a slope to the right. The path then rises and falls as it crosses little becks - with duckboards in places - before reaching a stone wall next to a wide track.

An information board gives details of animal, plant and bird life in the woodland - including sessile oak, wood anemone, woodcock, nut hatch, weasel, hedgehog and pied flycatcher.

We turn right along the track to pass through the gate and then walk downhill beside the stone wall before turning right over the spillway bridge. Continuing across the barrage, we soon pass the valve tower and reach a viewpoint - with a fish cage in the near distance on the reservoir. There are fine views across the reservoir - with Backstone Bank Wood prominent away on the right.

Continuing across the barrage, we reach the public road and turn right to follow the roadside verge back to our starting point in the car park close to the fishing lodge.

Shincliffe & Durham City

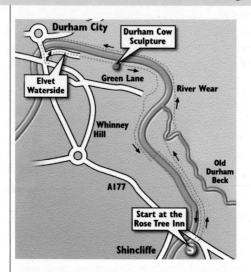

WEARDALE & THE RIVER WEAR

Superb views of majestic Durham City

Start: Rose Tree Inn, Shincliffe.

Distance: 3.25 miles.

Going: Level on wide riverside footpaths.

Refreshments: Rose Tree Inn & venues in Durham City.

Map: Ordnance Survey Landranger 88: Tyneside and Durham area.

84

THE CITY of Durham has a majestic look about it - and the banks of the River Wear offer the chance to take in some superb views.

Starting from the Rose Tree Inn at Shincliffe, we cross the A177 with care to follow the wide trackway that runs directly ahead with the river close at hand on the left. A field covers ground on the right before we reach soccer pitches and there are more pitches across the river as we continue along the riverbank.

There is an impressive suspension footbridge along this stretch of the river, but we bear diagonally to the right across the sports field to cross a metal footbridge over the Old Durham Beck.

The track soon passes between the sides of an old brick-built railway bridge and we then bear left beside the beck which soon joins the main river channel.

As the river bends to the left we see the rowing club premises on the opposite bank.

Regatta time on the River Wear

As we continue along the riverbank, Pelaw Wood covers the slope on our right-hand side and there are fine views of Durham's castle and cathedral directly ahead.

After crossing a brick bridge with metal rails, we continue along the tarmac path to pass Baths Bridge. The Prince Bishops Shopping Centre is prominent on the right and, after making our way under the arch of the bridge, we head up a flight of steps on the left that lead to Elvet Bridge. An information panel on the bridge states that it was built on the orders of Bishop Puiset in the late 12th century.

After crossing the bridge we bear left at the Swan And Three Cygnets to make our way back down to the riverside and along Elvet Waterside. The roadway runs under an arch of the Royal County Hotel and we then pass the swimming pool on the right-hand side.

The riverside path then runs beside a stone wall and the route has a brick surface as we continue past sports pitches. A splendid sculpture - Durham Cow - occupies a prominent position on the riverbank and we then pass a bandstand before following the bend round to the right.

As the gravel area curves to the right close to the rowing club we turn left across the tarmac roadway and pass through an area of pine woodland. We then turn left towards the riverbank and go on to make our way between the sides of an old railway bridge before passing the Hollow Drift rugby ground close on the right.

The track then runs around the bottom of Maiden Castle Wood to reach a bridge and kissing gate where we turn left to link up with the footbridge across the River Wear. After crossing the bridge we turn right to make our way back along the riverbank to the A177 and our starting point.

Our walk offers fine views of Durham Cathedral

Frosterley South

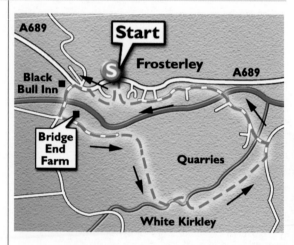

WEARDALE & THE RIVER WEAR

Where man has left his mark on the landscape

Start: Car park on north side of Frosterley's main street.

Distance: 4 miles.

Going: Well marked tracks wih one or two moderate gradients.

Refreshments: Venues in Frosterley.

Map: Ordnance Survey Landranger 92: Barnard Castle area.

L ARGE amounts of Frosterley marble appear in many County Durham churches and the quarries that provided the stone have left huge scars on the landscape on the south side of the town. A series of footpaths runs through this area to give a close look at man's impact on the countryside.

Starting from the car park on the north side of Frosterley's main street, we turn left and cross the road before making our way up the lane that leads to St Michael's Church. We walk past the church and through the churchyard to turn right along the pathway in front of the houses.

When the pathway divides, we walk left over the footbridge and continue directly ahead to the roadway before turning left down the slope past the Black Bull Inn on the right. We cross the road bridge and, just after the Primitive Methodist Church of 1861, we turn left along the lane with Old Bridge House on the right.

Passing close to the buildings at Bridge End Farm, we continue along the track with a hedge on the right-hand side and fence on the left. Beyond the field gate we can see the church spire across the river on the left and, as the track rises towards

Quarries scar the landscape south of Frosterley

St Michael's Church, Frosterley

farm buildings, we bear left at the waymarker on the fence. The well worn track leads to a kissing gate and then crosses the beck to run high above the River Wear. Just before the stile, though, we turn right to walk beside the wire fence.

There are extensive quarries on both sides of the pathway and, after crossing the latter stile, we continue up the left-hand edge of the field to reach another stile.

Keeping to the left - with the beck on the right - we cross another stile and then a footbridge of stone slabs and metal rails before heading up the slope. Opposite the bridge on the right, we turn left up the slope to make our way over another stile and then follow the left-hand field edge that soon runs between wire fences with quarries away on the left. At the next stile we walk directly ahead to join a gravel lane that soon bears left down the slope and then left again over the bridge.

The road veers to the right and we soon pass farm buildings on the right before another right-hand bend that leads to the level crossing. Continuing directly ahead we reach the main road and turn left towards Frosterley. As we reach the 30mph limit, bear left on the side road past St Ronan's Cottage on the left and a brick warehouse on the right.

Continuing past Allanton Mill on our right we walk beside the rail track and then pass through the gate into Mill Lane. We keep to the left, with Dene Hill high on the right and veer left past Western Hill to walk between a stone wall on the left and a wire fence on the right.

Passing through two kissing gates, we continue alongside the churchyard wall before making our way through the gap into the churchyard. On the other side of the churchyard we join the lane that leads to Front Street and turn left to return to our starting point at the car park.

Witton-le-Wear

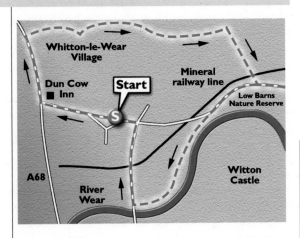

Whitton-le-Wear
Village

Dun Cow
■ Inn

Start

Mineral
railway line

Low Barns
Nature Reserve

A68

River
Wear

Witton
Castle

Walk Facts

WEARDALE & THE RIVER WEAR

Back to nature beside the busy A68

Start: Church of St Philip
and St James, Witton-le-
Wear.

Distance: 3.25 miles.

Going: Mainly field paths with
one or two moderate gradients.

Refreshments: Venues in
Witton-le-Wear.

Map: Ordnance Survey
Landranger 92: Barnard
Castle area.

MOST of us have bypassed Witton-le-Wear as we speed along the A68 near Hamsterley Forest, but it's worth stopping off to sample this lovely part of the County Durham countryside.

Starting from the church of St Philip and St James at the centre of the village, we walk along the main street with Carr's Terrace below on the left - and soon pass the Dun Cow Inn on the right. The footpath on the left side of the roadway continues past Witton Tower Gardens on the right and we return to the right-hand side before the junction with the A68.

We turn right to walk up the slope beside the A68 past a garage on the left and, opposite the bus stop, a raised driveway leads to a kissing gate next to a metal field gate. Continuing directly ahead for about 60 yards, we cross a stile and follow the right-hand edge of the field beside a wall and fence.

Farm buildings lie ahead as we walk towards a wooden kissing gate and then follow the left-hand edge of the next field to another gate. Our route runs straight on to a gap in the wall

Wildlife haven - Low Barns nature reserve

and through to a gravel track where we turn right to follow the trackway to the public road. Continuing across the road we head down the slope towards farm buildings and then pass through a metal gate on the left to follow the bottom edge of the field. After about 90 yards we cross a stile and head diagonally left across the field for about a third of the way down the field where a stile leads to a steeper bridge. Care is needed as the bridge was overgrown on my visit.

We walk along the top edge of the field to cross another stile and steeper bridge. As we continue directly ahead there are more farm buildings on the left and at the end of the field, we turn right to pass through a field gate and after two more fields we cross a stile close to the mineral railway line. After crossing with care we reach a gate next to the public road at Low Lane.

It's worth turning left here to walk along the section of roadway leading to Low Barns Nature Reserve, an area which used to be farm land and then gravel workings. It is now run by Durham Wildlife Trust with pleasant walkways running among stretches of water. There's an excellent coffee shop and exhibition area too.

Returning to the public road, we turn left and after passing a small section of housing, a detached residence, Wayside, is prominent on the right.

Look out for a small traction engine feature on a weather vane at properties on the right and just before the railway crossing we bear left along a track that soon runs beside the left-hand edge of the cricket field. A kissing gate in the left-hand corner leads to a path that follows the riverbank to the road bridge.

A gap in the wall leads to the public road where we turn right to make our way up the hill and under the railway bridge to return to our starting point at the church.

The Church of St Philip and St James, Witton-le-Wear

Notes

Notes

Notes